THE MIND OF THE
SOVIET FIGHTING MAN

THE MIND OF THE SOVIET FIGHTING MAN

A Quantitative Survey
of Soviet Soldiers,
Sailors, and Airmen

Compiled by
Richard A. Gabriel

Foreword by
J. L. Black

Greenwood Press
Westport, Connecticut • London, England

Library of Congress Cataloging in Publicaton Data

Gabriel, Richard A.
    The mind of the Soviet fighting man.

    1. Soviet Union—Armed Forces. 2. Soviet Union—
Armed Forces—Military life. I. Title.
UA770.G24 1984   355.1'0947   83-18520
ISBN 0-313-24187-2 (lib. bdg.)

Library of Congress Catalog Card Number: 83-18520
ISBN: 0-313-24187-2

First published in 1984

Greenwood Press
A division of Congressional Information Service, Inc.
88 Post Road West
Westport, Connecticut 06881

Printed in the United States of America

10 9 8 7 6 5 4 3 2

To my Aunt Evelyn Grieco who gave so much

CONTENTS

FOREWORD

Western scholars who study the Soviet armed forces face the same obstacles as do researchers on other dimensions of Soviet society, but scholars find these problems dramatically compounded by two further factors. In the first place, the normal complications of distance, language, and bureaucratic obstructionism are exacerbated by the element of secrecy which is characteristic of military matters everywhere but is particularly pervasive in the Soviet Union. Although there have been studies completed on the Soviet military establishment *per se*, equally competent works on Soviet militarism, and a large number of essays on Soviet military strategy, there have been few opportunities to examine in detail the vastly significant interplay of reciprocal influences between the Soviet military and Soviet society.

From the early 1920s, the Red Army has been regarded by Soviet authorities as an ideal medium through which social and political values might be disseminated to a widely dispersed and multinational population. Gradually —and especially after universal male conscription was introduced—the armed forces came to serve a multitude of nonmilitary social purposes, from raising the literacy level of the Soviet population to inculcating a nationwide political education. Thus, the Soviet military is more than the fighting arm of a state; it is also an important political and socializing agency. Moreover, when one studies the "human factor" of the Soviet military, the effectiveness of other instruments of socialization also are brought into question. The Komsomol, in which many recruits must have participated, is one such organization. More importantly, however, the efficacy of the paramilitary Society of Friends of Defense and Aviation-Chemical Construction (Osaviakhim—to 1948) and its successor organizations which together formed the Voluntary Society for Assisting the Army, Air Force, and Navy (DOSAAF) in 1952, might also be judged from studies of the soldiers themselves.

In light of the fact that the military remains an important economic component of the USSR, a significant cog in the socialization and Russification process, and an essential part of any integrationist policy in Eastern

Europe, our lack of precise information on the inner nature of the Soviet armed forces seriously handicaps our ability to predict what its collective behavior is likely to be in times of stress.

The second dilemma that faces scholars of the Soviet military is the simple fact that the USSR has been involved in too few conflicts since 1945 to allow one to observe its armed forces in action. I would be the last to recommend that the USSR fight more so that we can steal a peak at its practice sessions; suffice it to say that Warsaw Treaty Organization maneuvers tell us nothing about men in combat. Only in 1979, with the Soviet intervention in Afghanistan has it now become possible to make such observations—albeit through a very opaque glass.

Reports from and about the situation in Afghanistan are myriad. They range from commentaries on Soviet strategy and the degree to which its planners are able to adjust to unforeseen circumstances, to various charges and counter-charges about chemical warfare and acts of military terrorism against civilians. Recently, however, other kinds of reports have become available that address the important issues of troop morale and the implications of sustained conflict for the Soviet Home Front. Clearly, it is extremely difficult to verify reports about a contemporary crisis that is complicated by strong cross-currents of both traditional Cold War and more recent religious emotions. There is little enough hard evidence to corroborate even those accounts that logic tells us are sound.

About 300,000 soldiers and officers have been rotated from the Afghanistan Front, and, although military personnel sign pledges not to discuss their experiences with foreigners and even seem reluctant to discuss them at home, the war cannot help but raise questions about the morale and discipline of the Soviet armed forces. Soviet citizenry are not likely to query their government's presence in Afghanistan, especially to the degree that Americans questioned their government's actions in Vietnam. Nevertheless, scattered expressions of bitterness, frustration, and even horror inevitably will surface in the USSR—and sick and wounded young men are hard to conceal; so too is infectious hepatitis which some reports suggest has reached a near epidemic stage among recruits.

Only when participants from both sides are found in enough numbers and in a situation where natural biases and fears can be allayed will the story of Afghanistan be told accurately. But this may never be possible. For the present, however, we must make do with whatever means are open to us, and surveys of ex-Soviet servicemen of all ranks provide us with excellent means for judging what the attitudes of a young Soviet recruit in Afghanistan might be. The attitudinal data contained in the present study address in varying degrees of directness some of the very questions now being raised about Soviet troops who serve in Afghanistan: morale, unit cohesion, quality of life in the ranks, officer/troop relationships, ability to perform under stress, role and effectiveness of noncommissioned officers, and so on.

All serious scholars are aware of the problem areas of interview/question-

naire techniques. Questions that might lead the witness, selective interpretations of answers, and equally selective amnesia and/or imagination on the
part of the respondents, are all pitfalls for which the surveyor must be on
guard. "Western" scholars who interview "Eastern" subjects must also be
wary of language differences and how they may skew interpretations of
terminology. For a variety of understandable reasons, recent immigrants
may also be inclined to transmit answers that they assume will please the
interviewer. Professor Gabriel himself speaks to the potential of emigré
biases and forestalls the readers' concern that the credibility of his survey
might be affected by any of these considerations.

Richard A. Gabriel brings to this study the decided advantage of having
prepared and published the results of in-depth survey studies earlier. His
The New Red Legions: A Survey Data Source Book (1980) was a compila-
tion of responses from Soviet army veterans to some 160 questions about
every facet of military life. Gabriel's own analysis of these data appeared in
the same year as *The New Red Legions: An Attitudinal Portrait of the
Soviet Soldier*. As New England Director of the Inter-University Seminar
on Armed Forces and Society, a Fellow of the Canadian Institute of
Strategic Studies, an intelligence officer in the US Army Reserve, and
Vietnam veteran who has served on the staff of the Supreme Allied
Commander Europe at SHAPE, he can bring to these surveys both a personal
and professional understanding of the ways in which the military and
society are inextricably related.

The author's experience assures us that the right questions have been
asked. Other requisites help dispel any preconceived doubts about the
respondees: in the first place, the fact that the same questions were asked of
veterans of all three branches of the Soviet military—soldiers, airmen, and
sailors—provides an invaluable comparative check on the answers. Moreover, to my knowledge, these are the first surveys undertaken on the attitudes of Soviet sailors and airmen. In the second place, the rather recent
availability of a suitably large cross-section of emigrés from the USSR
provides both legitimacy in sampling size and in respondents who are at an
age when their answers still have current relevance. Finally, the anonymity of
a written questionnaire and the fact that it was printed in Russian, override
all doubts of the type mentioned above.

Readers will judge the usefulness of the material contained herein for
themselves. Indeed, the book's very purpose is to provide a basis for
research and judgment on the human factor within the Soviet military. In
short, Professor Gabriel's book is a valuable pioneering contribution to
Sovietology.

J. L. Black, Director
Institute of Soviet and East European Studies
Carleton University
Ottawa, Ontario

INTRODUCTION

Studying the Soviet military presents the researcher with a very difficult challenge. The nature of totalitarian social orders is such that one does not have ready access to the normal elements of information that constitute the spine of social science research. The problem is compounded when one attempts to examine an institution that the regime regards as vital to its existence. As a consequence, many of the efforts to include the Soviet military in studies of social institutions in the Soviet Union have had their analyses blunted by an inability to develop effective research approaches that could circumvent the existing obstacles to data collection.

This is even more true when the research involves the attitudes and feelings of the individuals who are members of those institutions—in this case, soldiers, sailors, and airmen. As a result, we know very little about important "human" factors in the military equation: morale, the degree of cohesion which can be expected of Soviet units, the quality of life within those units, the ability of units to perform under combat stress, the extent to which the officer corps is remote from its troops, the extent to which the NCO corps is able to perform adequately, and a whole range of other factors. An examination of these "informal" factors is crucial to the assessment of any military organization precisely because they act as inter-vening variables in the equation of combat effectiveness. Very clearly an army is something more than a group of individuals arranged in a row and decked out in uniforms. A military organization is primarily a fighting force, and the ability to fight is essentially a human, sociopsychological disposition that transcends the possession of the mere military and organi-zational means to engage in combat. Despite the importance of these intervening variables that comprise the human dimension of military force, the truth is that our knowledge of them within the context of the Soviet military remains limited.

There are a number of reasons why our knowledge of the human factors associated with military performance is so thin. In the first place we have lacked a fully developed theoretical framework for integrating the impact of these variables on combat performance. Despite the substantial contributions in this area by S.L.A. Marshall, Morris Janowitz, Edward Shills, Samuel Rolbant, and John Keegan, no complete theoretical model exists for integrating the impact of sociopsychological variables into an analytical framework for assessing the combat abilities of a military unit. In addition, the use in the West of economic and administrative models, analogies, techniques, and concepts to evaluate their own armies has led Western analysts to apply similar perspectives to their analyses of the Soviet military. This tendency has been encouraged further by the availability of official Soviet data that fits well into economic and administrative models. Thus a closed methodological circle began to evolve.

Yet another major reason why researchers have not focused directly upon the mind of the Soviet soldier and its range of sociopsychological variables is because they have not been able to acquire the relevant data. Until most recently researchers have not been able to gain access to Soviet soldiers in order to administer the kinds of questionnaires that could tap their attitudes and feelings. This inability has reenforced the tendency to focus upon other types of readily available information.

I undertook this work precisely because it seemed to me that much of the past work dealing with the mind of the Soviet soldier—what he knows, thinks, and feels—was lacking in empirical precision and that what was needed was a different kind of study. What was needed was a study that could proceed more empirically toward gathering the key elements of information dealing with a range of human sociopsychological factors that have been largely absent in past treatments of the Soviet military.

This work is unique in that it makes available for the first time the results of the first successful study in which relatively large numbers of Soviet soldiers, airmen, and sailors were interviewed in a systematic manner in order to obtain a new perspective on the Soviet military, namely as seen from within through the eyes of the Soviet soldier himself. It is the first attempt to "get inside the Soviet serviceman's head." A range of sociopsychological elements of comparison—the attitude structure of the Soviet serviceman, his feelings, his thoughts, and his evaluations—can be addressed along several dimensions. By using the survey approach to obtain sufficient numbers of in-depth and questionnaire interviews with Soviet soldiers, sailors, and airmen this study goes further than previous studies in making available for the first time a body of data that is drawn directly from the mind of the Soviet soldier. In this sense this study represents the first of its kind.

Method

Events conspired to aid in the successful completion of this work. In the past the flow of emigrés from the Soviet Union was merely a trickle and tended to consist largely of military defectors. Ten years ago as the Soviet Union adopted a somewhat more relaxed attitude toward emigration, that flow increased dramatically. Today approximately one half million emigrés have left the Soviet Union for new homes in Israel, Italy, Canada, and the United States. This human tide provides the researcher with an excellent opportunity to examine the Soviet military services through the eyes of its former members by employing empirical survey research techniques.

The argument for using this approach seems simple enough. In the Soviet Union military service is required of all citizens. All but approximately 12 percent of the conscript age males between eighteen and twenty-four actually serve in the military. It would stand to reason that the emigrés would also have served. Given that the emigré population reflects all age groups from young children to men over eighty, one would expect that a sample of emigrés would produce a group of respondents who performed their military service at various periods from 1945 to 1979. Further, if the Soviet conscript system is working as it should, then a sample of emigrés should contain a number of respondents who served in all branches of the military—army, navy, and air force—and they should be reasonably distributed as to the number of officers, noncommissoned officers, and enlisted men. A reasonable number should also have been commanders and occupied supervisory positions, and a reasonable number should have had combat experience while a reasonable number should not. In short, if the conscript system is working correctly, then a sample of those who have left the Soviet Union over the last ten years should contain as full a range of military experiences as would any other group of Soviet servicemen.

The sample selection process was direct. The first task was to open communications with sixty-four emigré service agencies in the United States, Italy, and Canada in order to seek their help in obtaining the names and addresses of recently arrived respondents. The objective was to contact the emigrés directly where possible and, where this was not possible, to use a mailed Russian-language questionnaire. In most cases the agencies agreed to provide what mailing lists they had or, as in other cases, to directly distribute the questionnaires themselves to respondents living within their area of responsibility. This second option was a concession to the desire for confidentiality. Using both methods 1,059 questionnaires were issued. The data collection period was set at three months although the study does incorporate data that kept coming in over a full year period. Four hundred direct-mail Russian language questionnaires were sent, while the remaining six hundred and fifty-nine were accepted by local service agencies for distribution to emigrés in their areas of responsibility.

At the end of the data collection period two hundred and seven questionnaires were returned or a response rate of 19.5 percent. Given most mail surveys this figure seemed somewhat low, because a normal rate of return for mail surveys runs closer to 30 percent. However, upon closer inspection of the data collection process it turns out that the rate of response relative to the actual potential universe exceeded 75 percent and is therefore acceptable for studies of this type.

Several factors combined to reduce the initial population selected for the survey. The 1,059 respondents was the number anticipated *assuming* that all of the questionnaires given to the service agencies were distributed by them; it also *assumed* that all the addresses obtained from these agencies for use in direct mail were accurate and current. Reality is never neat, and both these assumptions proved invalid. Many, indeed, most addresses provided turned out to be incorrect or out-of-date. In a country as mobile as the United States any respondent who had lived within it for seven years could be statistically expected to move at least twice. Since the post office forwards mail to new addresses for only six months, anyone who had moved even once over the seven-year period would most likely not receive a direct mail questionnaire. Moreover, we had no control over the local service agencies. Upon examination it seems clear that some agencies did send out the questionnaires, and some did not. Even when questionnaires were sent by the agencies often their own address lists proved inaccurate or out-of-date as well.

Taken together these difficulties reduced the initial population to be surveyed by almost 75 percent or by 794 of the original 1,059 respondents who had even a small chance that they would receive the questionnaire. Thus, the actual number of respondents who did receive the survey instrument or who were contacted directly for a face-to-face interview was reduced to 265. Of that number, 207 responded constituting a valid response rate of 78.1 percent of the *eligible* population, a response rate well within the valid parameters for any mail survey. Of the 207 respondents, 113 reported military service in the army, 39 in the navy, and 55 in the air force. It is these respondents who constitute the data base for this study.

Biases

Given the fact that the sample is accurately representative of the experiences of the Soviet serviceman it is appropriate to address a question that goes to the heart of the study. That question concerns the fact that the respondents in the sample are emigrés. The argument is raised that as emigrés they may not be typical of Soviet citizens and, as such, their views of the military may be biased. Furthermore, their emigré status may imply a high degree of social alienation that might also bias their perceptions of military life. Thus, it can be argued that the sample may reflect a body of data that is unalterably biased. How valid is this argument?

A response to the question of bias is to suggest that if the sample is indeed biased than an examination of the pages and pages of raw data should reveal the presence of certain "lumps" that can be expected to appear among the response profiles of certain questions. Such, an examination must show that the data are biased in the same direction if the argument is to have merit. A thorough examination of the data reveals no extreme bulges. By and large the respondents tend to spread rather "normally" in a statistical sense throughout the range of questions indicating that their responses are as "normal" as can be expected from any randomly selected sample. In any case only one of two logical positions regarding such a statistical analysis is acceptable. Either one assumes that a sample of emigrés is biased in the direction of a negative view of military service, or the sample is biased in the direction of a positive view. The only other alternatives are that the data are reasonably unbiased or randomly distributed. Given the absence of statistical lumps, if it is assumed that the bias is negative, then positive responses concerning military experience cannot be explained. The reverse is also true. In any case, an analysis of the data does not reveal any meaningful statistical idiosyncracies. It most certainly does not reveal any kind of consistent statistical bias along any discernible dimension.

Organization

Researchers do not very often have an opportunity to make their source material available to other interested scholars. Fortunately, this book provides an opportunity to make the first systematic, empirical, survey research study dealing with the feelings and attitudes of Soviet soldiers, sailors, and airmen available to the ranks of interested historians, military sociologists, psychologists, and defense analysts. The data are presented in raw tabular form, and accordingly, this book bears a strong organizational resemblence to what Arthur S. Banks and Robert B. Texter tried to do when they published their *Cross-Polity Survey*.

This volume is divided into three major sections each one respectively addressing the Soviet soldier, sailor, and airman. Each section contains within it raw data tables detailing the answers of respondents to eighty-one questions asked on the Russian-language questionnaire. Each set of data is further divided into the following twelve categories each addressing questions concerning various aspects of military service in each of the Soviet military branches: (1) General Views of Military Service, (2) Military Life, (3) Combat Ability, (4) Training, (5) The Quality of Officers and NCOs, (6) Leadership, (7) Morale and Discipline, (8) Ideology, (9) Unit Cohesion, (10) Desertion and AWOL, (11) Alcohol Use, and (12) Suicide. By making the raw data available in a single book it is hoped that it will generate increased interest among scholars to produce further studies.

Conclusion

This book suggests that one can learn much about the Soviet military by talking to its soldiers, sailors, and airmen and inquiring about their attitudes and military experiences. This argument would be accepted without question if it were possible to conduct a systematic survey of all the different groups that comprise the Soviet state. Because this is not possible, having to use a group of available respondents will, no doubt, raise questions regarding the validity of their perceptions. I suggest that emigré status *per se* does not necessarily remove members of this group from consideration as valid observers of their own military experience or as recorders of their own feelings and attitudes. In the end, of course, there is no way to remove all bias from any sample. However, the statistical analysis of the data suggests that whatever biases are extant in this sample are not debilitating. The ground is firm enough to support the assertion that the data are generally accurate.

In the final analysis it is clear that this study represents the only extant systematic empirical examination of the attitudes and experiences of Soviet soldiers, sailors, and airmen undertaken in the last five decades. No claim is made that it is definitive or that the data are totally free from error. The only claim put forth for it is that this work represents data that are available, systematic, empirical, generally representative, largely reliable, and, therefore, useful. Until Soviet authorities allow researchers to undertake similar studies within the Soviet Union—something which even democracies often find difficult to allow—surveys of the available data most suffice.

THE MIND OF THE
SOVIET FIGHTING MAN

THE SOVIET SOLDIER

General Views on Military Service

Table 1

If you could have avoided going into the
military like some people did would you
have avoided it?

	Yes	78	69.0%
	No	33	29.2%

N-111   Excluded: 2

Table 2

How did your family feel about your going into the military?

Thought it was my duty	7	6.2%
Thought it was a good thing	6	5.3%
Were generally not happy with my going	7	6.2%
Had no real feeling about it	2	1.8%
Resigned because it could not be avoided	86	76.1%
Were proud that I was serving my country	1	.9%

N-109   Excluded: 4

_____

Table 3

Did your friends think that going into the military was a good thing, something to be proud of, or something that could not be avoided?

A good thing	5	4.4%
Something to be proud of	6	5.3%
Something that could not be avoided	100	88.5%

N-111   Excluded: 2

Table 4

At the time you were in the military did you think it was a waste of time?

Yes	94	83.2%
No	16	14.2%

N-110   Excluded: 3

Table 5

Do you think you got anything good out
of going in the military?

	Yes	31	27.4%
	No	78	69.0%

N-109   Excluded: 4

Table 6

In general was your service in the military
a pleasant or unpleasant experience?

	Pleasant	18	15.9%
	Unpleasant	91	80.5%

N-109   Excluded: 4

Perceptions of Military Life

Table 7

Was military life more difficult than you
expected?

Yes	65	57.5%
No	46	40.7%

N-111   Excluded: 2

Table 8

Is the lack of space and privacy a major
complaint among the soldiers?

Yes	54	47.8%
No	51	45.1%

N-105   Excluded: 8

Table 9

In your experience in the military were certain
national and religious groups singled out for
unfair treatment?

Yes	78	69.0%
No	32	28.3%

N-110   Excluded: 3

Table 10

Was this a common practice?

Yes	64	56.6%
No	36	31.9%

N-100   Excluded: 13

Table 11

Generally, do most civilians treat soldiers
well when the soldier is away from his base?

Yes	92	81.4%
No	16	14.2%

N-108   Excluded: 5

Table 12

Did you ever hear of anyone in your unit selling
state property to get some extra money?

Yes	78	69.0%
No	33	29.2%

N-111   Excluded: 2

Training

Table 13

On a scale of from 1 to 10 in which one is
the worst and ten is the best, how would you
rate the military training your unit received?

1	6	5.3%
2	8	7.1%
3	14	12.4%
4	9	8.0%
5	20	17.7%
6	7	6.2%
7	**18**	**15.9%**
8	16	14.2%
9	3	2.7%
10	7	6.2%

N-113   Median Score: 5.2

Combat Ability

Table 14

In your opinion, how well do you think your unit
would have fought in actual combat?

Very well	10	8.8%
Fairly well	41	36.3%
Moderately well	38	33.6%
Poorly	16	14.2%
Very poorly	2	1.8%
N-107	Excluded: 6	

Table 15

On a scale of from 1 to 10 in which one is the
worst and ten is the best, how well do you think
your unit would do in actual combat?

1	3	2.7%
2	2	1.8%
3	18	15.9%
4	17	15.0%
5	17	15.0%
6	13	11.5%
7	16	14.2%
8	13	11.5%
9	2	1.8%
10	6	5.3%

N -113   Median Score: 5.0

Quality of Officers and NCOs

Table 16

Given the general quality of officers that
you served with in your military service,
how would you rate their quality as officers?

Extremely good	1	0.9%
Good	11	9.7%
Average	64	56.6%
Fair	16	14.2%
Poor	17	15.0%
Very poor	2	1.8%

N -111   Excluded: 2

The Soviet Soldier

Table 17

How would you rate the quality of non-commissioned
officers you came into contact with?

Extremely good	2	1.8%
Good	21	18.6%
Average	50	44.2%
Fair	23	20.4%
Poor	10	8.8%
Very poor	5	4.4%

N-110   Excluded: 2

Table 18

Did your officers/ncos always set the example
for their men?

	Yes	No	
Officers:	23.9%	65.5%	N-101
NCOs:	16.0%	65.5%	N-82

Table 19

Did your officers/ncos have the kind of judgement you would trust in combat?

	Yes	No	
Officers:	24.8%	66.4%	N-103
NCOs:	14.2%	66.4%	N-91

Table 20

Would your officers/ncos make good men to go into combat with?

	Yes	No	
Officers:	19.5%	66.4%	N-97
NCOs:	15.1%	66.4%	N-92

Table 21

Were your officers/ncos good examples for young soldiers?

	Yes	No	
Officers:	20.4%	61.1%	N-92
NCOs:	23.0%	61.1%	N-95

Table 22

Were your officers/ncos overly ambitious at the expense of his subordinates and his unit?

	Yes	No	
Officers:	51.3%	31.0%	N-93
NCOs:	42.4%	31.0%	N-83

Table 23

Did your officers/ncos seem more concerned with their own career advancement than with their men?

	Yes	No	
Officers:	72.5%	12.4%	N-96
NCOs:	49.5%	12.4%	N-70

Table 24

Did your officers/ncos try to avoid taking
responsibility when things went wrong?

	Yes	No	
Officers:	59.3%	23.9%	N-94
NCOs:	55.8%	23.9%	N-90

Table 25

Would your officers/ncos probably distort reports
to make themselves look better?

	Yes	No	
Officers:	46.9%	33.6%	N-91
NCOs:	48.7%	33.6%	N-93

Table 26

Did your officers/ncos seem more concerned
about the troops than his own advancement?

	Yes	No	
Officers:	11.5%	85.8%	N-110
NCOs:	8.9%	85.8%	N-107

Table 27

Did your officers/ncos use their positions
to take advantage of other soldiers?

	Yes	No	
Officers:	54.0%	26.5%	N-101
NCOs:	49.5%	26.5%	N-86

Table 28

In general, do soldiers feel that they can go
to their officers or sargents with a complaint
about being treated unfairly?

Yes	38	33.6%
No	72	63.7%

N-110   Excluded: 3

Leadership

Table 29

Did your officers/ncos share hardships with their men?

	Yes	No	
Officers:	22.1%	50.4%	N-82
NCOs:	38.9%	50.4%	N-101

Table 30

Did your officers/ncos go out of their way to show an interest in their men?

	Yes	No	
Officers:	28.3%	61.1%	N-101
NCOs:	15.9%	61.1%	N-87

Table 31

Did your officers/ncos see to it that their men had the things they needed in military life?

	Yes	NO	
Officers:	37.2%	43.4%	N-91
NCOs:	26.5%	43.4%	N-79

Table 32

Did your officers/ncos truly know their men and respect their capabilities?

	Yes	No	
Officers:	29.2%	57.5%	N-98
NCOs:	17.7%	57.5%	N-85

Table 33

Did your officers/ncos often praise their troops for doing a good job and mean it?

	Yes	No	
Officers:	37.2%	54.9%	N-104
NCOs:	17.7%	54.9%	N-82

Table 34

Were your officers/ncos willing to support their subordinates when they made mistakes?

	Yes	No	
Officers:	16.8%	78.3%	N-107
NCOs:	12.4%	78.3%	N-103

Table 35

Did your officers/ncos help their men overcome their lack of confidence?

	Yes	No	
Officers:	22.1%	54.9%	N-87
NCOs:	26.5%	54.9%	N-92

Table 36

Did your officers/ncos stick to the letter of his superiors orders?

	Yes	No	
Officers:	59.3%	30.1%	N-101
NCOs:	50.4%	30.1%	N-91

Table 37

Did your officers/ncos hesitate to take actions in the absence of instructions from their superiors?

	Yes	No	
Officers:	51.3%	32.7%	N-95
NCOs:	50.4%	32.7%	N-94

Table 38

Did your officers/ncos stifle the initiative
of others?

	Yes	No	
Officers:	38.0%	46.0%	N-95
NCOs:	35.3%	46.0%	N-92

Table 39

Did your officers/ncos tend to blame others
for things they were supposed to do when they
went wrong?

	Yes	No	
Officers:	48.6%	33.6%	N-93
NCOs:	48.6%	33.6%	N-93

Table 40

Were your officers/ncos selfish?

	Yes	No	
Officers:	54.3%	33.6%	N-100
NCOs:	50.4%	33.6%	N-95

Morale and Discipline

Table 41

Did you officers seem to care very much about
the morale of your unit?

            Yes   66   58.4%

            No   43   38.1%

    N-109   Excluded: 4

───

Table 42

Were your officers/ncos concerned about the unit's
morale and did they do everything they could to
make it high?
                              Yes   No

        Officers: 45.1%   49.6%   N-107

        NCOs: 20.3%   49.6%   N-79

───

Table 43

Did anyone in your unit ever physically assault an officer?

	Yes	41	36.3%
	No	69	61.1%

N-110   Excluded: 3

Table 44

Did anyone in your unit ever physically assault a non-commissioned officer?

	Yes	71	62.8%
	No	40	35.4%

N-111   Excluded: 2

Table 45

Have you heard stories about other units where officers have been assaulted?

	Yes	65	57.5%
	No	45	39.8%

N-110   Excluded: 0

Table **46**

How often do sargents treat the troops
unfairly?

Very often	27	23.9%
Often	37	32.7%
Seldom	33	29.2%
Rarely	8	7.1%
Almost never	3	2.7%

N-108   Excluded: 5

Table 47

How often do more experienced soldiers
treat new recruits unfairly?

Very often	42	37.2%
Often	36	31.9%
Seldom	23	20.4%
Rarely	4	3.5%
Almost never	3	2.7%

N-108   Excluded: 5

Table 48

Are the officers aware of the unfair treatment
that soldiers receive from other older soldiers?

         Yes   95   84.1%

         No   10   8.8%

N-105   Excluded: 8

Table 49

Does this have a negative effect on the
soldier's morale?

         Yes   86   76.1%

         No   19   16.8%

N-105   Excluded: 8

Table 50

Did you ever hear stories about soldiers who
were forced to give some of their pay to other
soldiers or to non-commissioned officers?

         Yes   34   30.1%

         No   76   67.3%

N-110   Excluded: 3

Ideology

Table 51

In your opinion, how important do you think that belief in an ideology--Marxism-Leninism--is in motivating a soldier to fight well?

The most important factor	10	8.8%
A very important factor	11	9.7%
Not very important at all	19	16.8%
Almost totally unimportant	71	62.8%

N-111   Excluded: 2

Table 52

Which of the following things do you think is most
important to motivating a soldier to fight well?

Close ties to his comrades in the unit	23	20.4%
Support of the friends back home	19	16.8%
Feeling that one's officers/ ncos care about you	5	4.4%
Belief in an ideology	12	10.6%
Not wanting to appear a coward in front of your friends	50	44.2%

N-109   Excluded: 4

Table 53

Among the soldiers that you knew, do you think that
classes in political subjects and ideology are important in making a soldier want to be a good soldier?

Yes	23	20.4%
No	85	75.2%

N-103   Excluded: 5

Table 54

On a scale of from 1 to 10 in which one is the least
important and ten the most important, how important
is a soldier's belief in Marxism-Leninism in motivating him to fight well?

1	50	44.2%
2	18	15.9%
3	17	15.0%
4	4	3.5%
5	5	4.4%
6	2	1.8%
7	4	3.5%
8	3	2.7%
9	1	.9%
10	5	4.4%

N - 108   Median Score: 2.0

Unit Cohesion

Table 55

How strongly did you develop feelings of
pride and affection for your military unit?

Very strongly	2	1.8%
Strongly	5	4.4%
Moderately	9	8.0%
Not very strong	28	24.8%
Unit pride did not concern me much	25	22.1%
No feelings of pride at all	42	37.2%

N-111   Excluded: 2

Table 56

How close to your fellow soldiers did you
feel when you were in the military?

Very close	6	5.3%
Close	16	14.2%
Moderately close	33	29.2%
Not close at all	21	18.6%
I felt few bonds with them	35	31.0%

N-111   Excluded: 2

Table 57

Did you make any close friends while you
were in the military?

Yes	78	69.0%
No	35	31.0%

N-113   Excluded: 0

Table 58

About how many close friends did you have in
the military?

One	10	8.8%
Two	25	22.1%
Three	21	18.6%
Four	4	4.4%
Five	3	2.7%
Six or more	15	13.3%
None	34	30.1%

N-113   Excluded: 0

Table 59

Never developed personal ties with his men

	Yes	No	
Officers:	49.5%	41.6%	N-103
NCOs:	31.8%	41.6%	N-84

Table 60

Did your officers/ncos encourage strong ties with the military unit?

	Yes	No	
Officers:	39.7%	47.8%	N-94
NCOs:	18.6%	47.8%	N-75

Table 61

Were your officers/ncos genuinely interested in their men's personal problems?

	Yes	No	
Officers:	31.8%	56.6%	N-100
NCOs:	15.0%	56.6%	N-81

Table 62

Did your officers/ncos draw too strong a line
between themselves and his men; were they too
distant?

	Yes	No	
Officers:	63.7%	23.0%	N-98
NCOs:	34.5%	23.0%	N-65

Table 63

Did your officers/ncos treat people in an impersonal manner---like cogs in a machine?

	Yes	No	
Officers:	63.7%	23.0%	N-98
NCOs:	44.3%	23.0%	N-76

Table 64

Were your officers/ncos generally available to
their men to deal with their personal problems?

	Yes	No	
Officers:	29.2%	57.5%	N-98
NCOs:	26.6%	57.5%	N-95

Table 65

Did your officers/ncos tend to limit his
contact with his men?

	Yes	No	
Officers:	54.0%	38.1%	N-104
NCOs:	28.3%	38.1%	N-75

Table 66

Did your officers/ncos listen with genuine
sympathy to the problems of the troops?

	Yes	No	
Officers:	21.3%	69.0%	N-102
NCOs:	13.3%	69.0%	N-93

Table 67

Did your officers/ncos stand up for his men
when dealing with his superiors?

	Yes	No	
Officers:	26.5%	57.5%	N-95
NCOs:	18.5%	57.5%	N-86

Desertion and AWOL

Table 68

When you were in the military did anyone
in your unit ever desert?

       Yes   56   49.6%

       No   53   49.6%

N-109   Excluded: 4

Table 69

In general were the stories that you heard
about soldiers deserting,

Very common	8	7.1%
Common	19	16.8%
Generally uncommon	5	4.4%
Rare	53	46.9%
Almost never heard such stories	25	22.1%

        N-110   Excluded: 3

Table 70

How often did soldiers in your unit go absent
without leave?

Quite often	32	28.3%
Often	24	21.2%
Fairly often	24	21.2%
Not very much	15	13.3%
Rarely	12	10.6%
Almost never	5	4.4%

N-112   Excluded: 1

Table **71**

What are some of the reasons that soldiers tried
to go absent without leave?

To get vodka	94	83.2%
To meet women	7	6.2%
To escape military life for a short time	6	5.3%
To escape military life for good	0	0
Family problems	0	0
Unfair treatment by superiors	0	0
To buy some extra food	0	0
To get some drugs	0	0

N-108   Excluded: 5

Table 72

Were your superiors concerned about the
problem of soldiers going absent without
leave?

Yes	79	69.9%
No	27	23.9%

N-106   Excluded: 7

Table 73

Were they concerned about the problem
of desertion?

Yes	73	64.6%
No	30	26.5%

N-103   Excluded: 10

Table 74

In general, is going absent without leave a
big problem in the military?

Yes	87	77.0%
No	20	17.7%

N-107   Excluded: 6

Table 75

Is desertion a big problem in the military?

Yes	54	47.8%
No	51	45.1%

N-105   Excluded: 8

Alcohol Abuse

Table 76

Do superior officers regard excessive drinking
as a major problem in the military?

	Yes	75	66.4%
	No	31	27.4%

N-106   Excluded: 7

Table 77

Did the amount of drinking in your unit affect
the ability of your unit to perform its mission?

	Yes	34	30.1%
	No	70	61.9%

N-104   Excluded: 4

Table 78

How often are ordinary soldiers drinking or
drunk while on duty?

Very often	6	5.3%
Often	12	10.6%
Seldom	29	25.7%
Rarely	30	26.5%
Almost never	32	28.3%
N-109	Excluded: 0	

Suicide

Table 79

When you were in the military did anyone in
your unit ever commit suicide?

Yes	55	48.7%
No	56	49.6%

N-111   Excluded: 2

Table 80

Did anyone in your unit ever attempt to commit
suicide?

Yes	60	53.1%
No	47	41.6%

N-107   Excluded: 6

Table 81

Did you ever hear stories about people committing suicide in other units?

Yes	95	84.1%
No	16	14.2%

N-111   Excluded: 2

Table 82

How common were the stories about suicide and
suicide attempts?

Very common	7	6.2%
Common	17	15.0%
Generally uncommon	20	17.7%
Fairly rare	44	38.9%
Almost never	19	16.8%

N-107   Excluded: 6

Table 83

In your experience whenever you heard about suicide
in the military did it happen most when:

The soldier first came into the military	27	23.9%
After he had been with his unit for awhile	67	59.3%

N-94   Excluded: 19

Table 84

Is it true that many suicide attempts are
actually attempts to get a release from
military service?

        Yes   55   48.7%

        No   35   31.0%

N-90   Excluded: 23

Table 85

In your experience, were your superiors concerned about the problem of suicide?

        Yes   54   47.8%

        No   40   35.4%

N-94   Excluded: 19

THE SOVIET AIRMAN

General Views on Military Service

Table 86

If you could have avoided going into the military
like some people did, would you have avoided it?

YES	40	72.7%
NO	15	27.3%

N-55   Excluded: 0

Table 87

How did your family feel about your going into
the military?

Thought it was my duty	5	9.1%
Thought it was a good thing	5	9.1%
Were generally not happy with my going	0	0
Had no feeling about it	0	0
Resigned because it could not be avoided	45	81.8%
Were proud that I was serving my country	0	0

N-55   Excluded: 0

Table 88

Did your friends think that going into the military
was a good thing, something to be proud of, or
something that could not be avoided?

A good thing	10	18.2%
Something to be proud of	0	0
Something that could not be avoided	45	81.8%

N-55   Excluded: 0

Table 89

At the time you were in the military did
you think that it was a waste of time?

Yes	40	72.7%
No	15	27.3%

N-55   Excluded: 0

Table 90

Do you think you got anything good out
of going in the military?

Yes	30	54.5%
No	25	45.5%

N-55   Excluded: 0

Table 91

In general was your service in the military
a pleasant or unpleasant experience?

Pleasant:	20	36.4%
Unpleasant:	35	63.6%

N-55   Excluded: 0

Perceptions of Military Life

Table 92

Was military life more difficult than you
expected?

Yes   20   36.4%

No   35   63.6%

N-55   Excluded: 0

Table 93

Is the lack of privacy and space a major complaint among the soldiers?

Yes   30   54.5%

No   25   45.5%

N-55   Excluded: 0

Table 94

In your experience in the military were certain
national and religious groups singled out for
unfair treatment?

Yes	40	72.7%
No	15	27.3%

N-55   Excluded: 0

Table 95

Was this a common practice?

Yes	24	43.6%
No	31	56.4%

N-55   Excluded: 0

Table 96

Generally do most civilians treat soldiers
well when the soldier is away from his base?

Yes	54	98.2%
No	1	1.8%

N-55   Excluded: 0

54

Table 97

Did you ever hear of anyone in your unit selling state property to get some extra money?

Yes	35	63.6%
No	20	36.4%

N-55   Excluded: 0

Combat Ability

Table 98

In your opinion, how well do you think your
unit would have fought in actual combat?

Very well	5	9.1%
Fairly well	30	54.6%
Moderately well	5	9.1%
Poorly	15	27.6%
Very poorly	0	0.0%

N-55   Excluded: 0

Table 99

On a scale of from 1 to 10 in which one is the worst
and ten is the best, how well do you think your unit
would do in actual combat?

1	0	0%
2	5	9.1%
3	10	18.2%
4	0	0%
5	5	9.1%
6	0	0%
7	10	18.2%
8	0	0%
9	15	27.6%
10	10	18.2%

Mean Score: 7.4   N-55

Training

Table 100

On a scale of from 1 to 10 in which one is the worst
and ten is the best, how would you rate the military
training your unit received?

1	0	0
2	0	0
3	15	27.6%
4	0	0
5	5	9.1%
6	5	9.1%
7	5	9.1%
8	5	9.1%
9	15	27.6%
10	5	9.1%

Mean Score: 7.2   N-55

Quality of Officers and NCOs

Table 101

Given the general quality of officers that you
served with in **your** military service, how would
you rate their quality as officers?

Extremely good	0	0
Good	20	36.4%
Average	20	36.4%
Fair	10	18.1%
Poor	5	9.0%
Very poor	0	0
N-55	Excluded: 0	

Table 102

How would you rate the quality of the non-commissioned
officers you came into contact with?

Extremely good	5	9.1%
Good	10	18.2%
Average	25	45.5%
Fair	14	25.5%
Poor	1	1.8%
Very poor	0	0
N-55	Excluded: 0	

- Yo

Table 103

Did your officers/ncos always set the example for their men?

	Yes	No	
Officers:	29.1%	61.8%	N-50
NCOs:	27.3%	61.8%	N-49

Table 104

Did your officers/ncos have the kind of judgement you would trust in combat?

	Yes	No	
Officers:	36.4%	56.4%	N-51
NCOs:	16.4%	56.4%	N-40

Table 105

Would your officers/ncos make good men to go into combat with?

	Yes	No	
Officers:	47.3%	52.7%	N-55
NCOs:	20.0%	52.7%	N-40

Table 106

Were your officers/ncos good examples to young soldiers?

	Yes	No	
Officers:	36.4%	54.5%	N-50
NCOs:	27.3%	54.5%	N-45

Table 107

Were your officers/ncos overly ambitious at the expense of his subordinates and his unit?

	Yes	No	
Officers:	70.9%	9.1%	N-44
NCOs:	63.6%	9.1%	N-40

Table 108

Did your officers/ncos seem more concerned with their own career advancement than with his men?

	Yes	No	
Officers:	54.6%	18.2%	N- 40
NCOs:	44.3%	18.2%	N- 35

Table 109

Did your officers/ncos often try to avoid taking
responsibility when things went wrong?

	Yes	No	
Officers:	61.8%	29.1%	N-50
NCOs:	43.6%	29.1%	N-40

Table 110

Would your officers/ncos probably distort reports
to make themselves look better?

	Yes	No	
Officers:	72.7%	27.3%	N-55
NCOs:	81.8%	18.2%	N-55

Table 111

Did your officers/ncos seem more concerned about their
troops than their own advancement?

	Yes	No	
Officers:	29.1%	70.9%	N-55
NCOs:	20.0%	70.9%	N-50

Table 112

Did your officers/ncos ever use their position to take
advantage of other soldiers?

	Yes	No	
Officers:	81.8%	18.2%	N-55
NCOs:	63.6%	18.2%	N-45

Table 113

In general do soldiers feel that they can go to
their officers or sargeants with a complaint about
being treated unfairly?

Yes	21	38.2%
No	34	61.8%

N-55   Excluded: 0

Leadership

Table 114

Did your officers and ncos share hardships
with their troops?

	Yes	No	
Officers:	38.2%	61.8%	N-55
NCOs:	18.2%	61.8%	N-44

Table 115

Did your officers/ncos go out of their way to show
an interest in their men?

	Yes	No	
Officers:	40.0%	60.0%	N- 49
NCOs:	10.9%	60.0%	N- 39

Table 116

Did your officers/ncos see to it that their men
had the things they needed in military life?

	Yes	No	
Officers:	52.8%	38.2%	N-50
NCOs:	36.4%	38.2%	N-49

Table 117

Did your officers/ncos truly know their men and
respect their capabilities?

	Yes	No	
Officers:	27.3%	61.8%	N-49
NCOs:	20.0%	61.8%	N-45

Table 118

Did your officers/ncos often praise their troops
for doing a good job and mean it?

	Yes	No	
Officers:	45.5%	54.5%	N-50
NCOs:	9.1%	54.5%	N-35

Table 119

Were your officers/ncos willing to support their
subordinates when they made mistakes?

	Yes	No	
Officers:	7.3%	83.6%	N-50
NCOs:	16.4%	83.6%	N-51

Table 120

Did your officers/ncos help men to overcome
their lack of confidence?

	Yes	No	
Officers:	65.5%	25.5%	N-50
NCOs:	56.4%	25.5%	N-45

Table 121

Did your officers/ncos stick to the letter of their
superior's orders?

	Yes	NO	
Officers:	81.8%	18.2%	N-55
NCOs:	70.9%	18.2%	N-50

Table 122

Would your officers/ncos hesitate to take actions in the absence of instructions from his superiors?

	Yes	No	
Officers:	61.8%	38.2%	N-55
NCOs:	50.9%	38.2%	N-47

Table 123

Did your officers/NCOs stifle the initiative of others?

	Yes	No	
Officers:	63.7%	27.3%	N-50
NCOs:	54.6%	27.3%	N-45

Table 124

Did your officers/ncos tend to blame others for things they were supposed to do when they went wrong?

	Yes	No	
Officers:	90.9%	9.1%	N-55
NCOs:	72.7%	9.1%	N-45

Table 125

Were your officers/ncos selfish?

	Yes	NO	
Officers:	63.6%	18.2%	N-45
NCOs:	72.4%	18.2%	N-50

Morale and Discipline

Table 126

Did your officers seem to care very much
about the morale of your unit?

Yes	45	81.8%
No	10	18.2%

N-55   Excluded: 0

Table 127

Were your officers/ncos concerned about the unit's
morale and did   everything they could to make it high?

	Yes	No	
Officers:	56.4%	34.5%	N-50
NCOs:	47.3%	34.5%	N-45

Table 128

Did anyone in your unit ever physically
assault an officer?

| | Yes | 20 | 36.4% |
| | No | 35 | 63.6% |

N-55   Excluded: 0

Table 129

Did anyone in your unit ever physically
assault a non-commissioned officer?

| | Yes | 45 | 81.8% |
| | No | 10 | 18.2% |

N-55   Excluded: 0

Table 130

Have you heard stories about other units where
officers have been assaulted?

| | Yes | 20 | 36.4% |
| | No | 35 | 63.6% |

N-55   Excluded: 0

Table 131

How often do sargeants treat the troops unfairly?

Very often	0	0
Often	25	45.5%
Seldom	25	45.5%
Rarely	5	9.1%
Almost never	0	0
N-55		Excluded: 0

Table 132

How often do more experienced soldiers treat new recruits unfairly?

Very often	10	18.2%
Often	16	29.1%
Seldom	29	52.7%
Rarely	0	0
Almost never	0	0
N-55		Excluded: 0

Table 133

Are the officers aware of the unfair treatment
that soldiers receive from other older soldiers?

Yes	49	89.1%
No	6	10.9%

N-55   Excluded: 0

Table 134

Does this have a negative effect on the
soldier's morale?

Yes	35	63.6%
No	20	36.4%

N-55   Excluded: 0

Table 135

Did you ever hear stories about soldiers who
were forced to give some of their pay to other
soldiers or to non-commissioned officers?

Yes	10	18.2%
No	45	18.8%

N-55   Excluded: 0

Ideology

Table 136

In your opinion, how important do you think that
belief in an ideology--Marxism-Leninism--is in
motivating a soldier to fight well?

The most important factor	0	0
A very important factor	5	9.1%
Not very important at all	20	36.4%
Almost totally unimportant	29	54.5%

N-55   Excluded: 0

Table 137

Which of the following things do you think is <u>most</u>
important to motivating a soldier to fight well?

Close ties to his comrades in his unit	6	12.0%
Support of the friends back home	25	50.0%
Feeling that one's officers/ncos care about you	19	38.0%
Belief in an ideology	0	0
Not wanting to appear a coward in front of your friends	0	0

N-50   Excluded: 5

Table 138

Among the soldiers that you knew, do you think
that classes in political subjects and ideological
indoctrination are important to making a soldier
want to be a good soldier?

	Yes	11	20%
	No	44	80%

N-55   Excluded: 0

Table 139

On a scale of from 1 to 10 in which one is the
least important and ten is the most important,
how important is a soldier's belief in Marxism-
Leninism in motivating him to fight well?

1	25	45.5%
2	15	27.6%
3	5	9.1%
4	5	9.1%
5	5	9.1%
6	0	0
7	0	0
8	0	0
9	0	0
10	0	0

Mean Score: 2.3   N-55

Unit Cohesion

Table 140

How strongly did you develop feelings of pride
and affection for your military unit?

Very strongly	6	10.9%
Strongly	0	0
Moderately	5	9.1%
Not very strongly	15	27.3%
Unit pride did not concern me much	5	9.1%
No feelings of pride at all	24	43.6%

N-55   Excluded: 0

Table 141

How close to your fellow soldiers did you feel
when you were in the military?

Very close	5	9.1%
Close	15	27.3%
Moderately close	10	18.2%
Not close at all	5	9.1%
I felt few bonds with them	20	36.4%

N-55   Excluded: 0

Table 142

Did you make any close friends while you
were in the military?

	YES	45	81.8%
	N O	10	18.2%

N-55   Excluded: O

Table 143

About how many close friends did you have
in the military?

One	20	40%
Two	20	40%
Three	O	0%
Four	O	0%
Five	O	0%
Six or more	10	20%

N-50   Excluded: 5

Table **144**

Never developed close ties with his men

	Yes	No	
Officers:	72.8%	20.0%	N-51
NCOs:	43.7%	20.0%	N-35

Table 145

Did your officers/ncos encourage strong ties with the military unit?

	Yes	No	
Officers:	65.5%	27.3%	N-51
NCOs:	63.7%	27.3%	N-50

Table 146

Were your officers/ncos genuinely interested in his men's personal welfare?

	Yes	No	
Officers:	34.5%	40.0%	N-41
NCOs:	25.5%	40.0%	N-36

Table 147

Did your officers/ncos draw to strong a line between themselves and their men; were they too distant?

	Yes	No	
Officers:	61.8%	27.3%	N-49
NCOs:	36.4%	27.3%	N-35

Table 148

Did your officers/ncos treat people in an impersonal manner--like cogs in a machine?

	Yes	No	
Officers:	69.1%	21.8%	N- 50
NCOs:	52.7%	21.8%	N- 41

Table 149

Were your officers/ncos generally available to the men to deal with their personal problems?

	Yes	No	
Officers:	36.4%	56.4%	N-51
NCOs:	25.5%	56.4%	N-45

Table 150

Did your officers/ncos tend to limit their contact
with their men?

	Yes	No	
Officers:	61.9%	36.4%	N-55
NCOs:	38.2%	36.4%	N-41

Table 151

Did your officers/ncos listen with genuine
sympathy to the problems of the troops?

	Yes	No	
Officers:	54.6%	**45.5%**	N-50
NCOs:	27.3%	45.5%	N-40

Table 152

Did your officers/ncos stand up for their men when
dealing with superiors?

	Yes	No	
Officers:	30.9%	69.1%	N-54
NCOs:	1.8%	69.1%	N-39

Desertion and AWOL

Table 153

When you were in the military did anyone in your unit ever desert?

Yes   19   34.5%

No   36   65.5%

N-55   Excluded: 0

_____

Table 154

In general, were the stories that you heard about soldiers deserting,

Very common   6   12.0%

Common   9   18.0%

Generally uncommon   0   0

Rare   25   50.0%

Almost never heard   10   20.0%
such stories

N-50   Excluded: 5

_____

Table 155

How often did soldiers in your unit go
absent without leave?

Quite often	18	32.7%
Often	16	29.1%
Fairly often	11	20.0%
Not very much	5	9.1%
Rarely	5	9.1%
Almost never	0	0

N -55   Excluded: 0

Table 156

What are some of the most common reasons that
soldiers tried to go absent without leave?

To get vodka	6	10.9%
To meet women	20	36.4%
To escape military life for a short time	24	43.6%
To try to get away from the military for good	0	0
Family problems	5	9.1%
Unfair treatment by superiors	0	0
To be some extra food	0	0
To get some drugs	0	0

N-55   Excluded: 0

Table 157

Were your superiors concerned about the problem
of soldiers going absent without leave?

Yes	21	38.2%
No	34	61.8%

N-55   Excluded: 0

Table 158

Were they concerned about the problem of
desertion?

Yes   45   81.8%

No   10   18.2%

N-55   Excluded: 0

Table 159

In general, is going **absent** without leave
a big problem in the military?

Yes   **44**   88.0%

No   6   12.0%

N-50   Excluded: 5

Table 160

Is desertion a big problem in the military?

Yes   31   62.1%

No   19   38.0%

N-50   Excluded: 5

Alcohol Abuse

Table 161

Do your superior officers regard excessive
drinking as a major problem in the military?

Yes	39	70.9%
No	16	29.1%

N-55   Excluded: 0

Table 162

Did the amount of drinking in your unit affect
the ability of your unit to perform its mission?

Yes	31	56.4%
No	24	43.6%

N-55   Excluded: 0

Table 163

How often are ordinary soldiers drinking or drunk while on duty?

Very often	1	1.8%
Often	19	34.5%
Seldom	0	0
Rarely	30	54.5%
Almost never	5	9.1%
N-55	Excluded: 0	

Suicide

Table 164

When you were in the military did anyone in
your unit ever commit suicide?

Yes	30	54.5%
No	25	45.5%

N-55   Excluded: 0

Table 165

Did anyone in your unit ever attempt to
commit suicide?

Yes	25	45.5%
No	30	54.5%

N-55   Excluded: 0

Table 166

Did you ever hear stories about people
committing suicide in other units?

Yes	39	70.9%
No	16	29.1%

N-55   Excluded: 0

Table 167

How common were the stories about suicide and
suicide attempts?

Very common	1	2.0%
Common	19	38.0%
Generally uncommon	5	10.0%
Fairly rare	15	30.0%
Almost never	10	20%
N-50	Excluded: 5	

Table 168

In your experience whenever you heard about
suicide in the military did it happen most when:

The soldier first came into the army	20	36.4%
After he had been with his unit for awhile	35	63.6%
N-55	Excluded: 0	

Table 169

Is it true that many suicide attempts are
actually attempts to get a release from
military service?

	Yes	35	70.0%
	No	15	30.0%

N-50   Excluded: 5

Table 170

In your experience were your superiors
concerned about the problem of suicide?

	Yes	24	48.0%
	No	26	52.0%

N-50   Excluded: 5

THE SOVIET SAILOR

General Views on Military Service

Table 171

If you could have avoided going into the military
like some people did, would you have avoided it?

Yes	24	61.5%
No	15	38.5%

N-39   Excluded: 0

Table 172

How did your family feel about your going into
the military?

Thought it was my duty	0	0
Thought it was a good thing	0	0
Were generally not happy with my going	0	23.1%
Had no real feeling about it	0	0
Resigned because it could not be avoided	27	69.2%
Were proud that I was serving my country	3	7.7%

N-39   Excluded: 0

Table 173

Did your friends think that going into the military was a good thing, something to be proud of, or something that could not be avoided?

A good thing	O	O
Something to be proud of	O	O
Something that could not be avoided	39	100.0%

N-39   Excluded: 0

Table 174

At the time you were in the military did you think that it was a waste of time?

Yes	36	92.3%
No	3	7.7%

N-39   Excluded: 0

Table 175

Do you think you got anything good out of
going in the military?

Yes   15   38.5%

No   24   61.5%

N-39   Excluded: 0

_____

Table 176

In general was your service in the military
a pleasant or unpleasant experience?

Pleasant   11   28.2%

Unpleasant   28   71.8%

N-39   Excluded: 0

_____

Perceptions of Military Life

Table 177

Was military life more difficult than you expected?

	Yes	30	76.9%
	No	9	23.1%

N -39   Excluded: 0

Table 178

Is the lack of privacy and space a major complaint among the soldiers?

	Yes	21	53.8%
	No	18	46.2%

N -39   Excluded: 0

Table 179

In your experience in the military were certain
national and religious groups singled out for
unfair treatment?

| | Yes | 15 | 38.5% |
| | No | 24 | 61.5% |

N-39   Excluded: 0

Table 180

Was this a common practice?

| | Yes | 22 | 56.4% |
| | No | 17 | 43.6% |

N-39   Excluded: 0

Table 181

Generally do most civilians treat soldiers well
when the soldier is away from his base?

| | Yes | 30 | 76.9% |
| | No | 9 | 23.1% |

N-39   Excluded: 0

Table 182

Did you ever hear of anyone in your unit
selling state property to get some extra
money?

	Yes	21	53.8%
	No	18	46.2%

N-39   Excluded: 0

Combat Ability

Table 183

In your opinion, how well do you think your unit
would have fought in actual combat?

Very well	15	38.4%
Fairly well	9	23.0%
Moderately well	9	23.9%
Poorly	0	0
Very poorly	0	0
N-33	Excluded: 3	

Table 184

On a scale of from 1 to 10 in which one is the worst and ten is the best, how well do you think your unit would do in actual combat?

1	0	0
2	0	0
3	0	0
4	12	33.3%
5	6	16.6%
6	0	0
7	6	16.6%
8	3	8.3%
9	3	8.3%
10	6	16.6%
N-36	Mean Score:	6.4

Table 185

Given the general quality of officers that you
served with in your military service, how would
you rate their quality as officers?

Extremely good	3	7.6%
Good	6	15.3%
Average	15	38.4%
Fair	3	7.6%
Poor	3	7.6%
Very poor	0	0

N-33   Excluded: 3

Table 186

How would you rate the quality of non-commissioned
officers you came into contact with?

Extremely good	3	8.3%
Good	9	25.0%
Average	17	47.2%
Fair	7	19.4%
Poor	0	0
Very poor	0	0

N-36   Excluded: 3

Training

Table 187

On a scale of from 1 to 10 in which one is the worst
and ten is the best, how would you rate the military
training your unit received?

1	0	0
2	0	0
3	0	0
4	0	0
5	15	45.5%
6	0	0
7	6	18.2%
8	3	9.1%
9	0	0
10	9	27.2%

N-33   Mean Score: 7.0

Quality of Officers and NCOs

Table 188

Did your officers/ncos always set the example
for their men?

	Yes	No	
Officers:	30.8%	53.8%	N-33
NCOs:	38.5%	53.8%	N-36

Table 189

Did your officers/ncos have the kind of judgement
you would trust in combat?

	Yes	No	
Officers:	30.8%	53.8%	N-30
NCOs:	23.1%	53.8%	N-30

Table 190

Would your officers/ncos make a good man to go
into combat with?

	Yes	NO	
Officers:	30.8%	61.5%	N-36
NCOs:	30.8%	61.5%	N-36

Table 191

Were your officers/noos good examples for
young soldiers?

	Yes	No	
Officers:	33.3%	51.3%	N-33
NCOs:	33.4%	51.3%	N-36

Table 192

Were your officers/noos overly ambitious
at the expense of their subordinates and
unit?

	Yes	No	
Officers:	56.4%	35.9%	N-36
NCOs:	48.7%	35.9%	N-33

Table 193

Did your officers/noos seem more concerned
with their own career advancement than with
their men?

	Yes	No	
Officers:	59.0%	25.6%	N-33
NCOs:	29.9%	25.6%	N-24

Table 194

Did your officers/ncos often try to avoid
taking responsibility when things went wrong?

	Yes	NO	
Officers:	61.5%	30.8%	N-36
NCOs:	61.5%	30.8%	N-36

Table 195

Would your officers/ncos probably distort reports to make themselves look better?

	Yes	No	
Officers:	61.5%	38.5%	N-39
NCOs:	53.8%	38.5%	N-36

Table 196

Did your officers/ncos seem more concerned about
the troops than their own advancement?

	Yes	No	
Officers:	18.0%	74.4%	N-36
NCOs:	18.0%	74.4%	N-36

Table 197

Did your officers/ncos use their position to take advantage of other soldiers?

	Yes	No	
Officers:	61.5%	38.5%	N-39
NCOs:	53.8%	38.5%	N-27

Table 198

In general do soldiers feel that they can go to their officers or sargeants with a complaint about being treated unfairly?

Yes	26	66.7%
No	13	33.3%

N-39   Excluded: 0

Leadership

Table 199

Did your officers/ncos share hardships with his men?

	Yes	NO	
Officers:	48.7%	35.9%	N-33
NCOs:	56.4%	35.9%	N-36

Table 200

Did your officers/ncos go out of their way to show an interest in their men?

	Yes	NO	
Officers:	33.6%	53.8%	N-33
NCOs:	25.9%	53.8%	N-32

Table 201

Did your officers/ncos see to it that your
men had the things they needed in military
life?

	Yes	No	
Officers:	35.9%	41.0%	N-30
NCOs:	43.6%	41.0%	N-33

Table 202

Did your officers/ncos truly know their men and
respect their capabilities?

	Yes	No	
Officers:	56.4%	43.6%	N-39
NCOs:	33.3%	43.6%	N-30

Table 203

Did your officers/ncos often praise their troops
for doing a good job and mean it?

	Yes	No	
Officers:	38.5%	53.8%	N-36
NCOs:	30.8%	53.8%	N-36

Table 204

Were your officers/ncos willing to support their
subordinates when they made mistakes?

	Yes	No	
Officers:	15.4%	69.2%	N-33
NCOs:	23.1%	69.2%	N-36

Table 205

Did your officers/ncos help men overcome
their lack of confidence?

	Yes	No	
Officers:	46.2%	38.5%	N-33
NCOs:	46.0%	38.5%	N-35

Table 206

Did your officers/ncos stick to the letter of their
superior's orders?

	Yes	NO	
Officers:	97.5%	2.6%	N-39
NCOs:	82.1%	2.6%	N-33

Table 207

Did your officers/ncos hesitate to take actions
in the absence of instructions from his superiors?

	Yes	No	
Officers:	61.5%	23.1%	N-33
NCOs:	69.2%	23.1%	N-36

Table 208

Did your officer/ncos stiffle the initiative
of others?

	Yes	No	
Officers:	51.3%	48.7%	N-39
NCOs:	43.6%	48.7%	N-36

Table 209

Did your officers/ncos tend to blame others
for things he was supposed to do when they
went wrong?

	Yes	No	
Officers:	61.6%	38.5%	N-39
NCOs:	38.5%	38.5%	N-30

Table 210

Were your officers/ncos selfish?

	Yes	No	
Officers:	54.9%	38.2%	N-36
NCOs:	54.9%	38.2%	N-33

Morale and Discipline

Table 211

Did your officers seem to care very much
about the morale of your unit?

          Yes   29   74.4%

          No   10   25.6%

    N-39   Excluded: 0

Table 212

Were your officers/ncos concerned about the unit's
morale and did they do everything they could to
make it high?

	Yes	NO	
Officers:	43.6%	48.7%	N-36
NCOs:	30.8%	48.7%	N-31

Table 213

Did anyone in your unit ever physically assault and officer?

          Yes   11   28.2%

          No   28   71.8%

    N-39   Excluded: 0

Table 214

Did anyone in your unit ever physically assault a non-commissioned officer?

	Yes	18	46.2%
	No	21	53.8%

N-39   Excluded: 0

Table 215

Have you ever heard stories about other units where
officers have been assaulted?

	Yes	18	46.2%
	No	21	53.8%

N-39   Excluded: 0

Table 216

How often do sargeants treat the troops
unfairly?

Very often	6	16.7%
Often	8	22.2%
Seldom	14	38.9%
Rarely	5	13.9%
Almost never	3	8.3%

N-36   Excluded: 0

Table 217

How often do more experienced soldiers treat new
recruits unfairly?

Very often	14	35.9%
Often	12	30.8%
Seldom	5	12.8%
Rarely	2	5.1%
Almost never	6	15.4%

N-39   Excluded: 0

Table 218

Are the officers aware of the unfair treatment
that soldiers receive from other older soldiers?

Yes	32	82.1%
No	7	17.9%

N-39   Excluded: 0

Table 219

Does this have a negative effect on the soldier's morale?

Yes	33	84.6%
No	6	15.4%

N -39   Excluded: 0

Table 220

Did you ever hear stories about soldiers who were forced to give some of their pay to other soldiers or to noncommissioned officers?

Yes	9	23.1%
No	30	76.9%

N -39   Excluded: 0

Ideology

Table 221

In your opinion, how **important** do you think
that belief in an ideology--Marxism-Leninism--
is in motivating a soldier to fight well?

The most **important** factor	7	17.9%
A **very** important factor	9	23.1%
Not very important at all	5	12.8%
Almost totally unimportant	18	46.2%

N-39   Excluded: 0

Table 222

Which of the following things do you think is <u>most</u>
important to motivating a soldier to fight well?

Close ties to his comrades in his unit	8	22.2%
Support of the friends back home	5	13.9%
Feeling that one's officers/ ncos care about you	0	0
Belief in an ideology	6	16.7%
Not wanting to appear a coward in front of your friends	17	47.2%

N-36   Excluded: 3

Table 223

Among the soldiers that you knew, do you think that classes in political subjects and ideological indoctrination are important in making a soldier want to be a good soldier?

	Yes	13	33.3%
	No	26	66.7%

N-39   Excluded: 0

Table 224

On a scale of from 1 to 10 in which one is the least
important and ten is the most important, how important
is a soldier's belief. in Marxism-Leninism in motivating
him to fight well?

1	15	38.4%
2	3	7.6%
3	6	15.3%
4	0	0
5	6	15.3%
6	0	0
7	3	7.6%
8	0	0
9	0	0
10	6	15.3%

N-39   Mean Score: 3.8

Unit Cohesion

Table 225

How strongly did you develop feelings of pride
and affection for your unit?

Very strongly	7	18.9%
Strongly	1	2.7%
Moderately	0	0
Not very strong	21	56.8%
Unit pride did not concern me much	5	13.5%
No feelings of pride at all	3	8.1%

N -37   Excluded: 2

Table 226

How close to your fellow soldiers did you feel
when you were in the military?

Very close	3	8.3%
Close	6	16.7%
Moderately close	21	58.3%
Not close at all	2	5.6%
I felt few bonds with them	4	11.1%

N-36   Excluded: 3

Table 227

Did you make any close friends while you were
in the military?

| Yes | 24 | 61.5% |
| No | 15 | 38.5% |

N-39   Excluded: 0

Table 228

About how many close friends did you have in
the military?

One	9	23.1%
Two	6	15.4%
Three	3	7.7%
Four	3	7.7%
Five	0	0.0%
Six or more	18	46.2%

N-39   Excluded: 0

Table 229

Did your officers/ncos ever develop strong
personal ties with his men?

	Yes	No	
Officers:	69.2%	30.8%	N-39
NCOs:	43.6%	30.8%	N-29

Table 230

Did your officers/ncos encourage strong ties
with the military unit?

	Yes	No	
Officers:	66.7%	33.3%	N-39
NCOs:	35.9%	33.3%	N-27

Table 231

Were your officers/ncos genuinely interested in
their men's personal problems?

	Yes	No	
Officers:	35.9%	64.1%	N-32
NCOs:	23.1%	46.2%	N-27

Table 232

Did your officers/ncos draw too strong a line
between themselves and his **men**; were they too
distant?

	Yes	No	
Officers:	53.9%	23.1%	N-30
NCOs:	53.9%	23.1%	N-30

Table 233

Did your officers/ncos treat people in an impersonal manner--like cogs in a machine?

	Yes	No	
Officers:	30.8%	35.9%	N-26
NCOs:	56.4%	35.9%	N-38

Table 234

Were your officers/ncos generally available to their men to deal with their personal problems?

	Yes	No	
Officers:	46.2%	46.2%	N-36
NCOs:	38.5%	46.2%	N-33

Table 235

Did your officers/ncos tend to limit their contact with their men?

	Yes	No	
Officers:	51.3%	41.0%	N-36
NCOs:	43.6%	41.0%	N-33

Table 236

Did your officers/ncos listen with genuine sympathy to the problems of the troops?

	Yes	No	
Officers:	15.4%	69.2%	N-33
NCOs:	15.4%	69.2%	N-33

Table 237

Did your officers/ncos stand up for his men when dealing with his superiors?

	Yes	No	
Officers:	18.0%	61.5%	N-31
NCOs:	30.8%	61.5%	N-36

Table 241

What are some of the reasons that soldiers tried
to go absent without leave?

To get vodka	31	86.1%
To meet women	5	13.9%
To escape military life for a short time	0	0
To try to get away from military life for good	0	0
Family problems	0	0
Unfair treatment by superiors	0	0
To buy some extra food	0	0
To get some drugs	0	0

N-36   Excluded: 3

Table 242

Were your superiors concerned about the problem of
soldiers going absent without leave?

Yes	26	66.7%
No	13	33.3%

N-39   Excluded: 0

Table 243

Were your superiors concerned about the problem of desertion?

	Yes	27	69.2
	No	12	30.8%

N-39   Excluded: 0

Table 244

In general, is going absent without leave a big problem in the military?

	Yes	33	84.6%
	No	6	15.4%

N-39   Excluded: 0

Table 245

Is desertion a big problem in the military?

	Yes	34	87.2%
	No	5	12.8%

N-39   Excluded: 0

Desertion and AWOL

Table 238

When you were in the military, did anyone
in your unit ever desert?

Yes	26	66.7%
No	13	33.3%

N-39   Excluded: 0

Table 239

In general, were the stories that you heard
about soldiers deserting:

Very common	4	11.1%
Common	9	25.0%
Generally uncommon	0	0
Rare	17	47.2%
Almost never heard such stories	6	16.7%

N-36   Excluded: 3

Table 240

How often did soldiers in your unit go absent
without leave?

Quite often	15	41.7%
Often	7	19.4%
Fairly often	0	0
Not very often	6	16.7%
Rarely	8	22.2%
Almost never	0	0

                N-36   Excluded: 3

Alcohol Abuse

Table 246

Do superior officers regard excessive drinking
as a major problem in the military?

	Yes	24	61.5%
	No	15	38.5%

N-39   Excluded: 0

Table 247

Did the amount of drinking in your unit affect
the ability of your unit to perform its mission?

	Yes	18	46.2%
	No	21	53.8%

N-39   Excluded: 0

Table 248

How often were ordinary soldiers drinking or drunk while on duty?

Very often	6	15.4%
Often	4	10.3%
Seldom	9	23.1%
Rarely	3	7.7%
Almost never	17	43.6%
N-39		Excluded: 0

Suicide

Table 249

When you were in the military did anyone in your
unit commit suicide?

	Yes	15	38.5%
	No	24	61.5%

N-39   Excluded: 0

Table 250

Did anyone in your unit ever attempt to commit
suicide?

	Yes	25	64.1%
	No	14	35.9%

N-39   Excluded: 0

Table 251

Did you ever hear stories about people committing suicide in other units?

Yes	30	76.9%
No	8	22.9%

N-35   Excluded: 4

Table 252

How common were the stories about suicide and
suicide attempts?

Very common	3	8.3%
Common	2	5.6%
Generally uncommon	3	8.3%
Fairly rare	16	44.4%
Almost never	12	33.3%

N-36   Excluded: 3

Table 253

In your experience whenever you heard about
suicide in the military did it happen most
when:

    The soldier first came   19   48.7%
    into the military

    After he had been with   20   51.3%
    his unit for awhile

      N-39   Excluded: 0

Table 254

Is it true that many suicide attempts are
actually attempts to get a release from
military service?

       Yes   21   63.6%

       No   12   36.4%

    N-33   Excluded: 6

Table 255

In your experience, were your superiors concerned about the problem of suicide?

	Yes	27	77.1%
	No	8	22.9%

N-35   Excluded: 4

THE QUESTIONNAIRE

OPINION RESEARCH CENTER
Case #_____   MANCHESTER, NEW HAMPSHIRE

INSTRUCTIONS:

This questionnaire is designed to obtain your views
about your experiences in military service. All answers
are confidential and no identification of respondents
is possible. Answer all questions as truthfully as possible. There are no right or wrong answers. What is
important is your opinions and views about your personal
experiences.

1. How old are you now? _____

2. How old were you when you first went into
   military service? _____

3. How long did you stay in military service?

       1.( ) under one year
       2.( ) one year
       3.( ) less than two years
       4.( ) two years
       5.( ) more than two years (How many years?
             _____)

4. When were you in military service?

       From _____ To _____ (Years only)

5. What type of living area did you come from
   before you entered the military?

       1.( ) small rural village
       2.( ) small urban town
       3.( ) large city
       4.( ) medium size city

6. What was the highest level of education you
   achieved before you went into the military?

   _____

7. Did you obtain more education after you left
   military service?

       1.( ) Yes   2.( ) No

8. Did you learn any useful civilian skills while
   you were in the military?

       1.( ) Yes   2.( ) No

9. What part of the military were you in?

    1.( ) army
    2.( ) air force
    3.( ) navy
    4.( ) strategic rocket forces
    5.( ) air defense corps
    6.( ) construction troops
    7.( ) border guards
    8.( ) other: _____(specify)

10. What was the highest rank you attained?

    1.( ) private soldier
    2.( ) non-commissioned
    3.( ) warrant officer
    4.( ) officer

11. What was your actual rank title? _____

12. What type of military unit were you in?

    1.( ) infantry
    2.( ) tanks
    3.( ) artillery
    4.( ) rockets
    5.( ) rear support unit
    6.( ) staff unit
    7.( ) other:_____(specify)

13. Did you make any close friends while you were
    in the military?

    1.( ) Yes   2.( ) No

14. About how many close friends did you have in
    the military?

    1.( ) one
    2.( ) two
    3.( ) three
    4.( ) four
    5.( ) five
    6.( ) six or more

15. In general was your service in the military a
    pleasant or unpleasant experience?

    1.( ) pleasant
    2.( ) unpleasant

16. If you could have avoided going into the mili-
    tary like some people did, would you have
    avoided it?

    1.( ) Yes   2.( ) No

1'. How did your family feel about your going into
the military?

1.( ) thought it was my duty
2.( ) thought it was a good thing
3.( ) were generally not happy with my going
4.( ) had no real feeling about it
5.( ) resigned because it could not be avoided
6.( ) were proud that I was serving my country

18. Did your friends think that going into the military was a good thing, something to be proud of,
or something that could not be avoided?

1.( ) a good thing
2.( ) something to be proud of
3.( ) something that could not be avoided

19. At the time you were in the military did you
think that it was a waste of time?

1.( ) Yes   2.( ) No

20. Do you think you got anything good out of
going in the military?

1.( ) Yes   2.( ) No

21. Was military life more difficult than you
    expected?

1.( ) Yes   2.( ) No

22. About how much free time did you have to your-
self in an average week?

1.( ) only a few hours
2.( ) about a day
3.( ) almost none at all
4.( ) every minute was accounted for
5.( ) generally enough free time

23. Compared to what you were being paid before you
went into the military, was military pay more
or less?

1.( ) less   2.( ) more

24. Was your pay enough for your needs?

1.( ) Yes   2.( ) No

25. Did your family ever have to send you money
so that you could get by?

1.( ) Yes   2.( ) No

26. Was hot water available every day for showers
    in your military unit?

    1.( ) Yes   2.( ) No

27. Was the food in the military generally better
    or worse than in civilian life?

    1.( ) better
    2.( ) worse
    3.( ) about the same

28. Was the quality of food you received adequate?

    1.( ) Yes   2.( ) No

29. Was the amount of food you received adequate
    for your needs?

    1.( ) Yes   2.( ) No

30. In general, how would you describe the living
    quarters you lived in while in the military?

    1.( ) very good
    2.( ) good
    3.( ) adequate
    4.( ) poor
    5.( ) bad
    6.( ) very bad

31. In your experience was housing in the military
    generally better than what you were used to in
    civilian life?

    1.( ) Yes   2.( ) No

32. Were the toilets located inside the barracks
    or was it necessary to go outside?

    1.( ) inside
    2.( ) outside

33. Were the barracks normally warm enough in winter
    to keep you comfortable?

    1.( ) Yes   2.( ) No

34. Did anyone in your unit ever develop sores or
    carbuncles from having a poor diet?

    1.( ) Yes   2.( ) No

35. Did anyone in your unit ever develop any other illness because of improper or inadequate diet?

    1.( ) Yes   2.( ) No

36. How much did the troops complain about the food?

    1.( ) very much
    2.( ) often
    3.( ) seldom
    4.( ) rarely
    5.( ) almost never

37. Did you or anyone in your unit ever obtain extra food from sources outside the military?

    1.( ) Yes   2.( ) No

38. Was this a common practice?

    1.( ) Yes   2.( ) No

39. Did you ever hear of anyone in your unit selling state property to get some extra money?

    1.( ) Yes   2.( ) No

40. Were the troop barracks usually overcrowded?

    - 1.( ) Yes   2.( ) No

41. Was this the usual condition in most units that you know of?

    1.( ) Yes   2.( ) No

42. In your unit about how many soldiers lived in a single room?

    _____(specify number)

43. About how many square meters was the room? _____

44. Did you have enough space and privacy in your barracks?

    1.( ) Yes   2.( ) No

45. Is the lack of privacy and space a major complaint among the soldiers?

    1.( ) Yes   2.( ) No

46. Does this lack of space or privacy lead to frequent fights among the soldiers?

    1.( ) Yes   2.( ) No

47. Could you make some extra money in the military by trading or selling things to other soldiers or to civilians?

    1.( ) Yes   2.( ) No

48. While you were in the military were you able to save some money for when you returned to civilian life?

    1.( ) Yes   2.( ) No

49. In general how much did the troops complain about the pay they received?

    1.( ) very much
    2.( ) often
    3.( ) seldom
    4.( ) rarely
    5.( ) almost never

50. Did you ever hear stories about soldiers who were forced to give some of their pay to other soldiers or to non-commissioned officers?

    1.( ) Yes   2.( ) No

51. In the whole time you were in the military, how many times were you allowed to leave the base for your own recreation?

    _____(number of times)

52. Were you ever allowed to leave the base without the company of some higher ranking soldier to keep an eye on things?

    1.( ) Yes   2.( ) No

53. How many times? _____

54. During your time in the military were you able to meet women?

    1.( ) Yes   2.( ) No

55. How often did you get to meet women?

   1.( ) very often
   2.( ) often
   3.( ) seldom
   4.( ) rarely
   5.( ) almost never

56. Could you visit these women in places off the military base?

   1.( ) Yes   2.( ) No

57. Did soldiers have to leave the base without permission to see women?

58. How often did soldiers in your unit leave the base without permission to see women?

   1.( ) very often
   2.( ) often
   3.( ) seldom
   4.( ) rarely
   5.( ) almost never

59. If you were caught leaving the base without permission to visit a woman was the punishment generally harsh or lenient?

   1.( ) harsh
   2.( ) lenient

60. Did anyone in your unit ever physically assault an officer?

   1.( ) Yes   2.( ) No

61. Did anyone in your unit ever physically assault a non-commissioned officer?

   1.( ) Yes   2.( ) No

62. Did anyone in your unit ever physically assault a warrant officer?

   1.( ) Yes   2.( ) No

63. Have you heard stories about other units where officers have been assaulted?

   1.( ) Yes   2.( ) No

64. In your opinion, how well do you think your unit
    would have fought in actual combat.

    1.( ) very well
    2.( ) fairly well
    3.( ) moderately well
    4.( ) poorly
    5.( ) very poorly

65. Did your officers seem to care very much about
    the morale of your unit?

    1.( ) Yes   2.( ) No

66. In your experience would you say that soldiers
    drink more in the military than in civilian
    life?

    1.( ) more in the military
    2.( ) more in the civilian life

67. Do officers drink heavily?

    1.( ) Yes   2.( ) No

68. Did you ever hear of or see an officer drunk
    on duty?

    1.( ) Yes   2.( ) No

69. Did you ever hear of or see a non-commissioned
    officer drunk on duty?

    1.( ) Yes   2.( ) No

70. How often are ordinary soldiers drinking or
    drunk while on duty?

    1.( ) very often
    2.( ) often
    3.( ) seldom
    4.( ) rarely
    5.( ) almost never

71. Do superior officers regard excessive drinking
    as a major problem in the military?

    1.( ) Yes   2.( ) No

72. Did the amount of drinking in your unit affect
    the ability of your unit to perform its mission?

    1.( ) Yes   2.( ) No   3.( ) Probably did

73. Are the punishments for drinking on duty severe or generally lenient?

    1.( ) severe
    2.( ) lenient

74. In your experience in the military were certain national and religious groups singled out for unfair treatment?

    1.( ) Yes   2.( ) No

75. Was this a common practice?

    1.( ) Yes   2.( ) No

76. How often do more experienced soldiers treat new recruits unfairly?

    1.( ) very often
    2.( ) often
    3.( ) seldom
    4.( ) rarely
    5.( ) almost never

77. Does this have a negative effect on the soldiers morale?

    1.( ) Yes   2.( ) No

78. Are the officers aware of the unfair treatment that soldiers receive from other older soldiers?

    1.( ) Yes   2.( ) No

79. How often so sargeants treat the troops unfairly?

    1.( ) very often
    2.( ) often
    3.( ) seldom
    4.( ) rarely
    5.( ) almost never

80. In general do soldiers feel that they can go to their officers or sargeants with a complaint about being treated unfairly?

    1.( ) Yes   2.( ) No

81. Generally do most civilians treat soldiers well when the soldier is away from his base?

    1.( ) Yes   2.( ) No

82. In your opinion, how important do you think
    that belief in an ideology--Marxism-Leninism--
    is in motivating a soldier to fight well?

    1.( ) the most important factor
    2.( ) a very important factor
    3.( ) not very important at all
    4.( ) almost totally unimportant

83. Which of the following things do you think is
    most important to motivating a soldier to fight
    well? (CHOOSE ONLY ONE)

    1.( ) close ties to his comrades in the unit
    2.( ) support of the friends back home
    3.( ) feeling that one's officers/nco's care
          about you
    4.( ) belief in an ideology
    5.( ) not wanting to appear a coward in front
          of your friends

84. When you were in the military did anyone in
    your unit ever commit suicide?

    1.( )Yes   2.( ) No

85. Did anyone in your unit ever attempt to com-
    mit suicide?

    1.( ) Yes   2.( ) No

86. Did you ever hear stories about people com-
    mitting suicide in other units?

    1.( ) Yes   2.( ) No

87. How common were the stories about suicide and
    suicide attempts?

    1.( ) very common
    2.( ) common
    3.( ) generally uncommon
    4.( ) fairly rare
    5.( ) almost never

88. In your experience whenever you heard about
    suicide in the military did it happen most when:

    1.( ) the soldier first came into the army
    2.( ) after he had been with his unit for awhile

89. Whenever you heard stories about suicide or su-
    icide attempts, were there stories about officers
    as well?

    1.( ) Yes   2.( ) No

90. Non-commissioned officers?

    1.( ) Yes   2.( ) No

91. Warrant officers?

    1.( ) Yes   2.( ) No

92. Is it true that many suicide attempts are actu-
    ally attempts to get a release from military
    service?

    1.( ) Yes   2.( ) No

93. In your experience, were your superiors con-
    cerned about the problem of suicide?

    1.( ) Yes   2.( ) No

94. In your unit how many conscript nco's did you
    have?

    _____

95. How many professional nco's did you have?

    _____

96. How many officers? _____

97. How many warrant officers? _____

98 Given the general quality of officers that you
    served with in your military service, how would
    you rate their quality as officers?

    1.( ) extremely good
    2.( ) good
    3.( ) average
    4.( ) fair
    5.( ) poor
    6.( ) very poor

99. How would you rate the quality of the non-
    commissioned officers you came into contact with?

    1.( ) extremely good
    2.( ) good
    3.( ) average
    4.( ) fair
    5.( ) poor
    6.( ) very poor

100. How close to your fellow soldiers did you feel
     when you were in the military?

    1.( ) very close
    2.( ) close
    3.( ) moderately close
    4.( ) not close at all
    5.( ) I felt few bonds with them

101. How strongly did you develop feelings of pride
     and affection for your military unit?

    1.( ) very strongly
    2.( ) strongly
    3.( ) moderately
    4.( ) not very strong
    5.( ) unit pride did not concern me much
    6.( ) no feelings of pride at all

102. When you were in the military did anyone in
     your unit ever desert?

    1.( ) Yes   2.( ) No

103. Did you ever hear of an officer deserting?

    1.( ) Yes   2.( ) No

104. Did you ever hear of a warrant officer desert-
     ing?

    1.( ) Yes   2.( ) No

105. Did you ever hear of a non-commissioned officer
     deserting?

    1.( ) Yes 2.( ) No

106. In general, were the stories that you heard
     about soldiers deserting,

    1.( ) very common
    2.( ) common
    3.( ) generally uncommon
    4.( ) rare
    5.( ) almost never heard such stories

107. How often did soldiers in your unit go absent
     without leave?

    1.( ) quite often
    2.( ) often
    3.( ) fairly often
    4.( ) not very much
    5.( ) rarely
    6.( ) almost never

108 What are some of the reasons that soldiers
     tried to go absent without leave? (check three
     of the most common reasons).

     1.( ) to get vodka
     2.( ) to meet women
     3.( ) to escape military life for a short time
     4.( ) to try to get away from the military for
           good
     5.( ) family problems
     6.( ) unfair treatment by superiors
     7.( ) to buy some extra food
     8.( ) to get some drugs

109. Were your superiors concerned with the prob-
     lem of soldiers going absent without leave?

     1.( ) Yes   2.( ) No

110. Were they concerned about the problem of
     desertion?

     1.( ) Yes   2.( ) No

111. In general, is going absent without leave a
     big problem in the military?

     1.( ) Yes
     2.( ) No

112. Is desertion a big problem in the military?

     1.( ) Yes
     2.( ) No

113. Is the punishment for going absent without
     leave harsh or lenient?

     1.( ) harsh
     2.( ) lenient

INSTRUCTIONS:

Below are a series of statements that people have
used to describe their officers, non-commissioned officers, and warrant officers. As you read each statement, if you agree that it describes the officers you
knew, place a mark in the space marked "officers." If
it describes the non-commissioned officers you knew, mark
the space "non-commissioned officers" and if it describes
the warrant officers you knew, mark the space "warrant officers." If it describes all three types of superiors,
mark the space "all three". If the statement does not
describe any of your superiors, mark the space "not
applicable".

---

114. Was genuinely interested in his men's personal
     problems.

     1.( ) officer   5.( ) not applicable
     2.( ) non-commissioned officer
     3.( ) warrant officer
     4.( ) all three

115. Went out of his way to show an interest in his men.

     1.( ) officer   5.( ) not applicable
     2.( ) non-commissioned officer
     3.( ) warrant officer
     4.( ) all three

116. Seemed more concerned with his own career advance-
     ment than with his men.

     1.( ) officer   5.( ) not applicable
     2.( ) non-commissioned officer
     3.( ) warrant officer
     4.( ) all three

117. He treated people in an impersonal manner-- like cogs
     in a machine.

     1.( ) officer   5.( ) not applicable
     2.( ) non-commissioned officer
     3.( ) warrant officer
     4.( ) all three

118. Stood up for his men when dealing with his superiors.

     1.( ) officer   5.( ) not applicable
     2.( ) non-commissioned officer
     3.( ) warrant officer
     4.( ) all three

119. Criticised subordinates in front of others.

    1.( ) officers   5.( ) not applicable
    2.( ) non-commissioned officers
    3.( ) warrant officers
    4.( ) all three

120. Shared hardships with his troops.

    1.( ) officers   5.( ) not applicable
    2.( ) non-commissioned officers
    3.( ) warrant officers
    4.( ) all three

121. Saw to it that his men had the things they needed in military life.

    1.( ) officers   5.( ) not applicable
    2.( ) non-commissioned officers
    3.( ) warrant officers
    4.( ) all three

122. Always set the example for his men.

    1.( ) officers   5.( ) not applicable
    2.( ) non-commissioned officers
    3.( ) warrant officers
    4.( ) all three

123. Drew too strong a line between himself and his men; he was too distant.

    1.( ) officers   5.( ) not applicable
    2.( ) non-commissioned officers
    3.( ) warrant officers
    4.( ) all three

124. Had the kind of judgement I would trust in combat.

    1.( ) officers   5.( ) not applicable
    2.( ) non-commissioned officers
    3.( ) warrant officers
    4.( ) all three

125. Truly knew his men and respected their capabilities.

    1.( ) officers   5.( ) not applicable
    2.( ) non-commissioned officers
    3.( ) warrant officers
    4.( ) all three

126. Never developed close personal ties with his men.

    1.( ) officers   5.( ) not applicable
    2.( ) non-commissioned officers
    3.( ) warrant officers
    4.( ) all three

127. He was concerned about the unit's morale and did every-
     thing he could to make it high.

    1.( ) officers   5.( ) not applicable
    2.( ) non-commissioned officers
    3.( ) warrant officers
    4.( ) all three

128. Often tried to avoid taking responsibility when
     things went wrong.

    1.( ) officers   5.( ) not applicable
    2.( ) non-commissioned officers
    3.( ) warrant officers
    4.( ) all three

129. Listened with genuine sympathy to the problems of
     the troops.

    1.( ) officers   5.( ) not applicable
    2.( ) non-commissioned officers
    3.( ) warrant officers
    4.( ) all three

130. Often praised his troops for doing a good job and
     meant it.

    1.( ) officers   5.( ) not applicable
    2.( ) non-commissioned officers
    3.( ) warrant officers
    4.( ) all three

131. Would make a good man to go into combat with.

    1.( ) officers   5.( ) not applicable
    2.( ) non-commissioned officers
    3.( ) warrant officers
    4.( ) all three

132. He would probably distort reports to make himself
     look better.

    1.( ) officers   5.( ) not applicable
    2.( ) non-commissioned officers
    3.( ) warrant officers
    4.( ) all three

133. He was overly ambitious at the expense of his
     subordinates and his unit.

     1.( ) officers   5.( ) not applicable
     2.( ) non-commissioned officers
     3.( ) warrant officers
     4.( ) all three

134. Tended to concentrate on the small unimportant
     things.

     1.( ) officers   5.( ) not applicable
     2.( ) non-commissioned officers
     3.( ) warrant officers
     4.( ) all three

135. Encouraged strong ties with the military unit.

     1.( ) officers   5.( ) not applicable
     2.( ) non-commissioned officers
     3.( ) warrant officers
     4.( ) all three

136. Used his position to take advantage of other soldiers.

     1.( ) officers   5.( ) not applicable
     2.( ) non-commissioned officers
     3.( ) warrant officers
     4.( ) all three

137. Stifled the initiative of others.

     1.( ) officers   5.( ) not applicable
     2.( ) non-commissioned officers
     3.( ) warrant officers
     4.( ) all three

138. He was willing to support his subordinates when they
     made mistakes.

     1 ( ) officers   5.( ) not applicable
     2.( ) non-commissioned officers
     3.( ) warrant officers
     4.( ) all three

139. Seemed more concerned about the troops than his
     own advancement.

     1.( ) officers   5.( ) not applicable
     2.( ) non-commissioned officers
     3.( ) warrant officers
     4.( ) all three

140. He would hesitate to take actions in the absence
of instructions from his superiors.

    1.( ) officers   5.( ) not applicable
    2.( ) non-commissioned officers
    3.( ) warrant officers
    4.( ) all three

141. Tended to limit his contact with his men.

    1.( ) officers   5.( ) not applicable
    2.( ) non-commissioned officers
    3.( ) warrant officers
    4.( ) all three

142. He was generally available to his men to deal with
their personal problems.

    1.( ) officers   5.( ) not applicable
    2.( ) non-commissioned officers
    3.( ) warrant officers
    4.( ) all three

143. He was a good example to young soldiers.

    1.( ) officers   5.( ) not applicable
    2.( ) non-commissioned officers
    3.( ) warrant officers
    4.( ) all three

144. Helped men overcome their lack of confidence.

    1.( ) officers   5.( ) not applicable
    2.( ) non-commissioned officers
    3.( ) warrant officers
    4.( ) all three

145. He was selfish.

    1.( ) officers   5.( ) not applicable
    2.( ) non-commissioned officers
    3.( ) warrant officers
    4.( ) all three

146. Tended to blame others for things he was supposed to
do when they went wrong.

    1.( ) officers   5.( ) not applicable
    2.( ) non-commissioned officers
    3.( ) warrant officers
    4.( ) all three

147. Stuck to the letter of his superiors orders.

    1.( ) officers   5.( ) not applicable
    2.( ) non-commissioned officers
    3.( ) warrant officers
    4.( ) all three

    _____

148. About what percentage of non-commissioned officers
     that you knew in the military were conscript non-
     commissioned officers?

     _____

149. About what percentage of the non-commissioned officers
     that you knew in the military were professional,
     career-service non-commissioned officers?

     _____

150. In general, were conscript non-commissioned of-
     ficers better than professional non-commissioned
     officers?

     1.( ) yes   2.( ) no   3.( ) both about the same

151. On a scale of from 1 to 10 in which 1 is the worst
     and 10 is the best, how well do you think your unit
     would do in actual combat?

     ‾1‾ ‾2‾ ‾3‾ ‾4‾ ‾5‾ ‾6‾ ‾7‾ ‾8‾ ‾9‾ ‾10‾
     WORST   BEST
                    (check one)

152. About how many hours a week are spent in political
     subjects and ideological indoctrination?

     _____

153. Among the soldiers that you knew, do you think that
     these kinds of classes are important in making a
     soldier want to be a good soldier?

     1.( ) yes   2.( ) no

154. On a scale of from 1 to 10 in which 1 is the least
     important and 10 is the most important, how important
     is a soldier's belief in Marxism-Leninism in moti-
     vating him to fight well?

     ‾1‾ ‾2‾ ‾3‾ ‾4‾ ‾5‾ ‾6‾ ‾7‾ ‾8‾ ‾9‾ ‾10‾
     LEAST IMPORTANT   MOST IMPORTANT

155. Did Soviet authorities make any effort to break up strong personal ties between soldiers?

1.( ) yes   2.( ) no

156. On a scale of from 1 to 10 in which 1 is the worst and 10 is the best, how would you rate the military training your unit received?

1	2	3	4	5	6	7	8	9	10
WORST									BEST

About the Compiler

RICHARD A. GABRIEL is Professor of Politics at St. Anselm College. He is New England Director of the Inter-University Seminar on Armed Forces and Society, a Fellow of the Canadian Institute of Strategic Studies, and of the Mid-East Study Group at Hebrew University in Jerusalem. Dr. Gabriel is an intelligence officer in the U.S. Army Reserve and has held posts at Brookings Institution, the Directorate of Foreign Intelligence, and the U.S. Army Intelligence School. He is the author of *The Antagonists: A Comparative Combat Assessment of the Soviet and American Soldier* (1984), *Fighting Armies* (1983), *To Serve With Honor* (1982), and *The New Red Legions* (1980) published by Greenwood Press.

www.ingramcontent.com/pod-product-compliance
Lightning Source LLC
Chambersburg PA
CBHW070443100426
42812CB00004B/1193